BEING A *Gentle*man
A RESOURCE FOR MEN

Glenn Pickering

 Whole Person Associates Inc
Duluth, Minnesota

Whole Person Associates Inc
210 West Michigan
Duluth MN 55802-1908
218-727-0500

Scripture passages are taken from the Revised Standard Version of the Bible.

Being a *Gentle*man: A Resource for Men

Printed in the United States of America by Versa Press
10 9 8 7 6 5 4 3 2 1

Publisher: Donald A Tubesing
Editorial Director: Susan Gustafson
Assistant Editor: Patrick Gross
Designer: Joy Morgan Dey

Library of Congress Cataloging-in-Publication Data

Pickering, Glenn, 1953–
    Being a gentleman : a resource for men / Glenn Pickering.
      p. cm.
    ISBN 0-938586-75-0 (pbk.) : $12.95
    1. Men—Conduct of life.   I. Being a gentle man.   II. Title.
  BJ1601.P63   1993
  170'.81—dc20   93-9723

Dedication
This book is dedicated to Dick Scanlon,
whose gentleness, honesty, and perfect jump shot
all have enriched my life.

Acknowledgments

Since the things that I write flow directly out of my experiences with the people in my life, it literally would be true to say that I owe a debt of gratitude to every person with whom I ever have interacted. To all of you, I want to say "thanks."

In addition, I specifically want to thank those people who influenced me and this book in ways that were particularly profound and direct. Thank you, Gwen and Rachel, for the things that you taught me each day. Thank you, Don Tubesing and Susan Gustafson, for helping me to find the right way to structure this material. And thank you, Joel, Tom, Ernie, Phil, Paul, Greg, and Dave, the guys in my men's group, for your willingness to tell me the truth.

Preface

I was born to be a *gentle*man—a male person whose gentleness, caring, honesty, and faith in others would enable those others to be healed. The struggle to become this *gentle*man has not been an easy one for me. As with many men, my earlier years had taught me a lot more about the importance of power, ambition, and control than they had about mercy, humility, or love. Furthermore, I always had been extremely shy and more than a little afraid of being vulnerable. Consequently, the process of growing into my true self has been difficult at times, and more than a little painful.

However, it also has been a journey filled with wonder—a journey that has helped me to experience more fully the freedom, capacity for intimacy, and healing power that always had lurked just below my conventional male exterior. If I could give you just one gift, I would give to you the opportunity to experience the same sort of transformation that has allowed me to more fully claim my self.

Toward that end, I have chosen to share with you my most personal experiences and my reflections upon those experiences. I share these with you not because I foolishly believe myself to be unique but because I know that I am not. As Carl Rogers pointed out, it is that which is most personal which is most universal. I have chosen to share my most personal self with you, then, in the hope that you will recognize yourself in me and in the belief that this encounter with your deepest self will be both clarifying and challenging to you, as you strive to become a *gentle*man.

Until we meet again.

—Glenn

Contents

How to use this book

This book has a different arrangement from most others. Each chapter begins with a brief quote, one or two prose paragraphs that introduce the topic, and a brief affirmation/prayer. Then follow a sequence of aphorisms and a set of questions for your personal reflection. Because this book is different than most, I want to give you a few suggestions about how you might best use it.

Give yourself time to think
If you read this book as fast as I read most books, nothing of real consequence will occur. In this book, the overriding goal is to evoke a response in you—to help you to begin to think more clearly about yourself and about the subjects being raised. Therefore, it is important that you take the opportunity to pause after each passage, page, or topic (whichever works best) and to reflect upon the material contained therein.

Write notes to yourself
When you stop to reflect upon a particular passage, please jot down in one of the many spaces provided whatever thoughts, associations, and insights may occur to you. This will serve to clarify your thinking, to generate additional insights, and fortify your memory. The biggest compliment that you possibly could give me would be to write all over this book.

Share what you have written
I urge you to use this book as the basis of a study group or to find some other way in which to share your insights with others, because it is in teaching that we truly learn.

Use the *Questions for personal reflection*

Your reflections upon these questions can help you to apply the material to your own life and also can serve as the springboard for your discussions with others. Whether you are using the book individually or in a group setting, I urge you to read the questions carefully and to answer them in writing before you move on.

Use it your way

You have a number of options about the order in which you read the material and the use to which you put it. If you read the book on your own, for example, you certainly can read sequentially through the book, perhaps even at one sitting. However, you also can read one chapter at a time, read through the chapters in a different order, read the chapters at widely separate times, or use the book as a source of randomly chosen thoughts for the day, all without losing too much in the process.

Similarly, if you use the book in a group setting, members can discuss the entire book in one session, read and discuss one chapter per week, or select inspirational passages and talk about the visions triggered by those particular passages.

Let me hear from you

I love hearing from my listeners and readers—in many ways, that is my favorite part of speaking or writing. So please feel free to drop me a line. I still am very much in the process of learning, growing, and becoming, and I am sure that your feedback would be of great value to me.

On Control

Although the need for control often is confused with strength, in truth our controlling behaviors are born not out of strength, but out of weakness, fear, and desperation.

On Control

Dropping our active forms of control

My desire to be in control of things can be seen most clearly in my small behaviors, particularly in my knee-jerk reactions to certain situations. When my little girl runs down the hallway, my first instinct is to tell her not to, because I am afraid that she might get hurt. When my wife talks about quitting work at some point in the future, I panic for a second thinking about the money. When I see someone (especially a child) struggling at some task, I automatically start telling him or her how to do it, even though the person is not asking me for help. When I make a stupid mistake, my first reaction is to conceal that fact so that people will not think badly of me. When new policies are instituted at work, I sometimes respond negatively, just because I am afraid of change. And when a friend is making what seems to me to be a mistake, I am hard-pressed to keep my mouth shut.

All of these needless, knee-jerk reactions spring from my desire to control people and situations—from my wanting to make sure that everything turns out all right. This wanting to make sure everything turns out all right, in turn, is based on fear—fear of letting go, of the unknown, of what will happen if I am not in charge. In reality, of course, I am not in charge of anyone else's life, and my attempts to control the events and people around me create a great deal of needless stress for me and much frustration for those whose strivings for autonomy are stifled by my need for control.

I am not in control of others, I do not need to be in control of others, and I want to give up all of my foolish, self-serving attempts to remake everyone else in my own image.

When I talk myself into believing that I am responsible for someone else (for example, when I tell myself that it is my job to make sure that someone else makes the right decision or feels the right way), my simple little life becomes very complicated indeed.

What are the signs that I have made this mistake? When I find myself feeling confused, telling half-truths, taking on the problems of others, manipulating situations, or worrying excessively about people's reactions, I can be sure that I once again have erred in this way.

Many people (including myself, unfortunately) try to control their partners. We controllers try to get our partners to behave in certain ways or to make certain decisions, and then we call this nonsubtle form of manipulation "love."

There is a difference, however, between love and control. When I seek to control people, I try to force them to become the people that I want them to be. When I truly love them, I try instead to help them to become the people that they want to be.

True love requires that I drop all of my attempts to control people and that I strive instead to accept them for who they are.

When I believe that I desperately need a person to act in a certain way toward me, I no longer am free to love that person.

True love rules out the possibility of control; the two are, by definition, mutually exclusive.

Many people have said that God grants us free will, the implication being that God could have decided otherwise. It seems to me, though, that since God is love and since love rules out the possibility of control, God's relationship with us could not possibly have included a dimension of control.

We have free will, then, not because God *allows* us to, but because there is no other possibility.

My misguided attempts to control others almost always spring from a sincere desire to be helpful. There is a difference, however, between trying to control someone and trying to be helpful—to control is to provide help at times when no one is asking for it.

One problem with my need to be in control of others is that I never really am.

The only thing harder than relinquishing my control of others is acknowledging the fact that I never really had any to begin with.

Questions for personal reflection

1. What people and situations are most likely to trigger a controlling reaction in you?

2. How do people usually respond to your attempts to actively control their behavior?

3. If you were to drop all of your attempts to mold or influence others, how might that affect your relationships? How might that affect you?

On Control

Dropping our passive forms of control

Although passivity might appear to be the opposite of control (since passivity appears to involve the voluntary relinquishing of even the appropriate level of control), in reality passivity can be a very controlling response. For example, sometimes I passively go along with someone else's ideas, even though I do not really agree with them, because I am trying to make them like me—because I am trying to control their opinion of me. Sometimes I do not tell the truth because I am trying to avoid a confrontation—because I am trying to control the course of the conversation. Sometimes I appear to give in because I know that will help me to get my way—because I am trying to control the outcome of certain situations. And finally, sometimes I remain passive in relationships rather than actively sharing myself, because I am afraid of being vulnerable—because I am trying to control the risk that is involved in being fully alive.

I want to be less controlling of others and to be more actively in charge of my own life. I want to quit hiding my real self behind my "nice" facade and to quit worrying so much about what people will think.

Sometimes my silence is just another way to lie.

Although people often confuse the two, passivity ("whatever you want, honey") is not the same as love, because love requires that we actively give of ourselves.

All too often, passivity is either a way to avoid self-revelation or a silent form of control, and neither of these is love.

Passivity and aggression are similar in this way: they both eliminate the need to engage in honest self-revelation.

Passivity and aggression are merely different ways of protecting ourselves against the possibility of being vulnerable.

If I cannot be vulnerable, I cannot know love.

When I choose to blame others, I choose to remain passive.

When I choose to behave passively, I choose to blame others (or at least to retain that right). So when I choose to be passive, my partner never will feel loved or accepted by me.

When a man throws up his hands, says, "OK, OK, we'll go to the stupid party" and walks out of the room, he does his partner a threefold disservice: he implicitly retains the right to be critical of the decision if he does not enjoy the party (which he of course will not), he probably leaves his partner feeling angry and guilty, and he eliminates the possibility of engaging in the sort of negotiations that can lead to deeper intimacy.

At the risk of pointing out the obvious, this is not love.

When I truly love someone, I need to keep listening, talking, and negotiating until we both feel finished.

Questions for personal reflection

1. What are some of the passive ways in which you seek to control the responses of others?

2. What parts of yourself are you most likely to hide? What simple steps could you take to begin changing this pattern?

3. Think of the last time that you blamed somebody else for something. Looking at it more honestly, what part did you play in the problem? If you had acknowledged this at the time, how would you have felt and how might the interaction have been changed?

On Listening

Like all simple tasks, listening is incredibly difficult.

On Listening

The tendency to rehearse rather than listen

All too often, when we are supposed to be listening we really are busily rehearsing our response and impatiently waiting for a break in the conversation. Many of our discussions consist of nothing more than a whole sequence of these rehearsed responses. In such conversations, the interaction moves very quickly and predictably, no one really listens, everyone spends all of his or her nontalking time preparing defensive responses, very little gets accomplished, and everyone walks away feeling unheard.

When we truly are listening, on the other hand, we are fully present while the other person is talking. We therefore do not have the opportunity to prepare our response ahead of time, which means that when the other person finishes talking it probably will take us a moment to organize our thoughts into a meaningful reply. Such a conversation moves rather slowly and is punctuated by a number of pauses and silences. Although the slowness of the interaction can make it appear that very little is happening, in truth a great deal gets accomplished: people feel heard, new ideas are generated, and true intimacy begins to develop.

I do not need to rehearse while others are speaking. I need only to pay careful attention and to trust that, as a result of paying attention, I will indeed be able to generate a meaningful response when it is my turn to speak.

If in a particular conversation I always know what I am going to say next, I can be sure that I am not really listening.

Obviously, my tendency to rehearse my next response greatly interferes with my ability to listen. What might not be so obvious is that it also interferes with my ability to respond.

It is difficult to respond empathically and appropriately to a remark that I did not really hear.

The more quickly a conversation moves along, the less likely it is to be constructive.

I have found that I can gauge the current status of a marital relationship, in part, simply by noticing the speed at which the couple's conversations tend to move.

Questions for personal reflection

1. Are some people and/or situations particularly likely to make you want to rehearse your responses? What triggers this desire?

2. Think of a specific conversation during which you spent a lot of time rehearsing. What effect did your rehearsal have upon the conversation?

3. Some people who are trying to break the rehearsal habit find it helpful to truly focus their attention on what the other person is saying, or to allow for more pauses in the conversation, or to summarize the other person's comments before making their own. Would any of these techniques be of help to you?

On Listening

The tendency to talk too much

A number of times, at parties and other social situations, I have run into a person who so dominated a group's conversation that I have felt forced to choose between either rudely interrupting or passively withdrawing from the entire conversation. Unfortunately, there also have been times (during a lecture, in the midst of a conversation that was of great interest to me, or in the presence of a listener who put me up on a pedestal), when I suddenly have realized, much to my chagrin, that I have been behaving in a similar way.

When one person talks too much, the conversation never can become a discussion between two equals. I suspect that this fact explains both the irritation that I feel upon encountering a person who monopolizes the conversation and the frequency with which we men resort to this technique.

I do not need to be afraid to have a real encounter with someone. The next time that I meet someone, I want to try to communicate in a way that helps us to establish a truly equal relationship.

Many men are like lonely shut-ins; when given a chance to speak, they totally dominate the conversation.

When I talk too much, even I no longer can hear myself.

The problem with a monologue is that neither person really learns anything.

The more I grow as a person, the more difficult it is for me to listen to a lecture or to give a sermon.

The more words a person uses to make a point, the less likely I am to understand the point.

Perhaps the same could be said of the speaker, as well.

Some people use a lot of words because they are afraid of what will happen when they quit talking.

Questions for personal reflection

1. Think of a person whose tendency toward monologues is annoying to you. What, specifically, does this person do that prevents him or her from being a good conversationalist?

2. Given what you discovered in answering question #1, what might you want to do differently in your own conversations?

On Listening

The tendency to "fix" rather than listen

I have noticed that when we men try to be understanding listeners we often make the mistake of trying to move too quickly to the solution—the mistake of trying to fix things right away, without taking the time to really listen. For example, when my little girl tells me that one of her kindergarten classmates was mean to her, she does not need for me to respond by saying, "Well, just ignore her." What she needs is for me to listen—to really hear the confusion, pain, and hurt that she felt when her little friend was rude to her. If I can do that, she soon will feel safe enough, loved enough, and strengthened enough to begin to formulate her own action plan, and I will not need to fix anything.

I want to quit fixing people and to instead give them the one thing that they really need—my whole self.

A while ago, I was telling a friend of mine about an incident that had left me feeling sad and depressed. Instead of saying something like "I understand" or "That must have hurt," he said, "Go for a jog; that will lift your spirits." He solved my problem for me and thereby missed the point entirely.

We men were brought up to solve problems and to fix things. This approach works well when the car needs a tune-up, but it does not work nearly so well when a friend is in need. A friend is someone who needs to be heard, not someone who needs to be fixed.

Our friends need our love, not our answers.

All too often, we men choose to fix people rather than truly listen to them because we are trying to avoid having to feel their pain.

I can be of help to someone only if I first am willing to let myself acknowledge their current emotional state.

I often hear caring men say that it is hard for them to just listen to their partners when they are hurting. They want to help them—they want to do something to make them feel better. They do not understand that to listen is to be of great help.

The healing process begins the instant I feel understood.

When a client asks me, "How can I solve this problem?" I can be sure that he or she does not yet fully understand the problem.

It is not that hard to figure out how to fix something. Once all of the aspects of a given problem are fully understood, the solution to the problem generally becomes obvious. Of course, obvious is not the same as easy.

Before I can decide *how*, I have to know *what*.

God tells us what, not how.

The same could be said of a good friend.

Questions for personal reflection

1. When are you most likely to try to fix a situation instead of trying to listen attentively?

2. When you are talking, what do you want from your listener?

3. How might you get better at providing that type of response to others when it is your turn to listen?

On Telling the Truth

". . . and the truth will make you free."
(John 8:32)

On Telling the Truth

Acknowledging the truth about ourselves

There are several things I must do if I am to prepare my proverbial soil in such a way as to create the possibility of growth. The first of these involves the acknowledgment of my imperfections. Clearly, I cannot even begin the growth process until I am willing to acknowledge my current flaws.

Given this fact, one might think that I always would have been not only willing but even eager to recognize my weaknesses. Unfortunately, such was not the case. All too often, I chose to continue doing things in my same old way rather than to acknowledge the need for change. Obviously, this prevented me from changing—from becoming the *gentle*man that I was born to be.

In looking back at my prior attempts to mask my deficiencies, I wonder, why? Why did I try so hard to avoid acknowledging the problems that were so obvious to everyone else? Perhaps I was afraid of change. Perhaps it seemed unmanly to acknowledge my weaknesses.

For whatever reason, it took me a long time to discover the liberation and growth that can occur once I simply admit, to myself, that I am imperfect. And even now, it is tempting for me to act as if those imperfections do not really exist.

*I am not perfect, I need not pretend to be perfect,
and I want to get better at acknowledging, to myself
and to others, the many specific ways in which I am
imperfect.*

When I refuse to acknowledge the way things are, I forfeit my ability to change those things—I become my own jailer.

There is a great deal of power released when I say, "I want to get better."

To acknowledge what is, is to make change possible. That is why people cannot acknowledge the ways things are until they truly are ready to move on.

We humans are funny—we tend to deny our really major mistakes and to agonize over our trivial ones.

The harder my mind works at justifying a particular behavior, the surer I can be that there was indeed something wrong with the behavior.

In the long run, the only thing more painful than the acknowledgment of the truth is my refusal to acknowledge the truth.

It is very difficult to recover from a secret.

Unless I hear the truth, I never will be healed.

When my enemies tell me the truth, I am too busy defending myself to really listen. Thus, it is important that I allow my friends to tell me the truth.

Questions for personal reflection

1. What aspects of your personality are difficult for you to acknowledge, even to yourself?

2. To whom might you be able to confess some of these flaws?

3. Are there ways in which you actively discourage people from telling you the truth about yourself? Are there ways in which you could encourage them, instead?

4. With whom might you be able to start this process?

On Telling the Truth

Telling others the truth

My reluctance to tell other people what I am really thinking or feeling does great damage to my relationships—it leaves me with unspoken resentments, prevents other people from knowing as much about me as they otherwise could, and eliminates the possibility of true intimacy. I used to pretend to myself that I was being nice because I did not want to hurt people. Now I know, though, that I was being nice because I was afraid—afraid of how the other person would react if I told the truth.

Now I have found that when I do tell the truth to the people that I trust, one of three things generally happens: the person accepts the feedback with a minimum of fuss (contrary to my catastrophic expectations), gets a bit angry at first but later acknowledges the truth of what I said, or corrects my misunderstanding. At the risk of pointing out the obvious, I have no reason to fear any of these three outcomes.

My fears notwithstanding, it is important that I tell my trusted friends the truth, in the spirit of love, and I will strive to become as honest as I am affectionate.

Just as I need for my friends to tell me the truth about myself, so too must I be willing to be honest with them if I am to be their friend.

If I cannot be honest with someone (which includes my asking them the rather personal questions that tend to pop into my head), then we are not really friends.

If I am to be a friend, I must be willing to be honest, which requires that I be willing to go one step beyond being polite.

Jim and I always are very polite with one another, which suggests to me that he and I are destined to remain acquaintances.

All too often, I see myself trying to protect a relationship; I do not tell the other person how I feel or what I think, for example, because I do not want the other person to feel bad. Unfortunately, whenever I desire above all else to protect the other person, the list of topics that are off-limits grows steadily longer, until eventually there is no meaningful subject left that can be discussed.

Nothing will destroy a relationship more surely than my desire to protect it.

I now can see all too clearly that my past unwillingness to tell a certain person how unhappy I was in our relationship was born not out of niceness but out of cowardice.

I regret to the core my previous unwillingness to tell the truth.

Questions for personal reflection

1. In what relationships are you most likely to protect the other person, rather than tell the truth?

2. What have you gained by doing this?

3. What have you lost?

4. If you were to start telling some of these people the truth, what kinds of things might you want to tell them?

5. What person(s) in your life would be most open to hearing such things?

On Compromising

Whenever someone is winning, someone else is unhappy.

On Compromising

Compromising vs. having to win

We are not clones of one another. In any long-term relationship, certain differences of opinion will develop—differences that, if they are not dealt with correctly, will threaten the stability of the relationship. Such differences require that we learn the art of compromise—the art of listening carefully to one another and continuing to generate options until we find one that addresses each person's main concerns.

Unfortunately, in our culture, we find very few relationships in which compromise is the order of the day. As I see it, there are several reasons for this. The first is that very few people seem to understand what it means to compromise. Many people mistakenly see compromise as another word for appeasement, and therefore are not interested in learning the art of compromise. Furthermore, in our competitive culture, we are taught that we should play to win, and it can be difficult to lay that lesson aside long enough to negotiate an effective compromise. Finally, we also are taught to be impatient, which can make it difficult to tolerate the time-consuming process of finding the middle ground.

Thus, we always will be tempted to settle for being either the aggressor who demands to win or the passive doormat who volunteers to lose, because in the short run it is faster and easier to settle for these roles than it is to work at finding an effective compromise. In the long run, though, compromise truly is the most natural, fastest, and best way, because a true compromise eliminates the resentments, passive resistances, and rehashings that always occur when we try to move too quickly.

I no longer want to act as if my only two options are to be demanding or to give in. I want to find the middle way—the way that really works.

Being willing to stand up for myself ought not rule out the possibility of being patient and gentle with others.

Whenever I get excited about some idea of mine, I want to implement it immediately. I therefore get frustrated if other people are less than enthusiastic about my plans or voice opposition to my ideas. At such times, it is important for me to remember that I need not see someone else's opposition as a problem to be solved and that I always am free to let our disagreement serve as a catalyst for the development of a superior plan.

In other words, I must always remember that resistance is not an obstacle to be overcome but rather a sign that we have not yet finished our discussion.

The fact that my answer is right does not necessarily mean that yours is wrong.

Whenever I seek to impose my will upon something or someone else, I can be sure that I am overlooking a more natural solution.

When I quit fighting it or forcing it, the answer will come.

When I honestly desire to resolve an interpersonal problem in a way that will allow both of us to be treated fairly and lovingly, a multitude of possible solutions generally present themselves to me. Conversely, when I am not able to find a mutually acceptable solution, I can be quite sure that I am not allowing love to be my guide.

When my first order of business in a discussion is to win or to be right, the odds are against my ever finding a truly just solution.

If I have to win, then I can be sure that my proposed solution(s) will, in at least some small way, be detrimental to the relationship.

If I always play to win, then even when I win I lose.

If love is not the answer, then I am asking the wrong question.

We humans often ask the wrong question.

The decision to take turns winning does not constitute a compromise.

Questions for personal reflection

1. A couple once said to me, "We have hundreds of dumb arguments each week," to which I replied, "No, you have two or three dumb arguments, hundreds of times apiece." When we play to win, the issue under discussion never really gets resolved to everyone's satisfaction, which means that the same topic is likely to come up again and again.

   Which of your disagreements tend to get recycled?

2. When you can tell that you are beginning to have one of these disagreements, what might you say in place of your normal response (that is, trying to win or to be right)?

   (Note: Some people find it helpful to request a time-out, to make a process comment—"We are doing it again," to actively look for common ground, or to consciously choose to really listen.)

3. Who do you know who could serve as a good role model, in this regard?

On Compromising

Compromising vs. giving in

Consistently giving in is just as destructive to a relationship as is the need to win. When one person always gives in, he or she is being dishonest (which reduces the intimacy level in the relationship), is short-circuiting the interaction (which prevents the couple from ever developing the skills necessary for compromise), and is building up resentments that eventually will destroy the relationship. It takes two people to play the win-lose game—one who insists on winning and one who insists on losing—and if the game is to end, *both* people must be willing to change.

In the long run, passivity is no better than aggression; I want to become more honest and direct in my dealings with others.

In a relationship, it is indeed important that I be willing to bend. There is a difference, however, between being willing to bend and needing so badly to please someone else that I forfeit my own integrity.

When people do not think of themselves very much, pretty soon they do not think very much of themselves.

Jesus said that we should love people as ourselves, not instead of ourselves.

Sometimes, when I tell my clients that they need to become more assertive, that they need to ask themselves, "What do I want?" they respond by saying, "Oh, I couldn't do that; that would be selfish." They assume that their deepest needs are purely egocentric and that to be true to themselves would be to live lives characterized by total self-absorption.

In truth, however, if I am in touch with what I really want (that is, of what the deepest part of me wants), I realize that what I truly desire is to treat both myself and others in a loving way. Thus, when I ask myself, "What do I really want to do in this situation?" the solutions that come to me almost never are those that benefit only myself.

People often act as if the old adage "Be true to yourself" somehow contradicts the equally old adage "Do what is right." In truth, however, these two sayings are merely different ways of expressing the same advice.

Since God resides in my core, to be profoundly moral requires only that I be true to my deepest self.

To be absolutely true to myself in any given instant is to get a glimpse of the next world.

Questions for personal reflection

1. When some people think of the word *compromise,* they picture someone acting like a doormat. What do you picture?

2. What might be a more helpful way in which to conceptualize the process?

3. Some people who previously played a very passive role in their lives are reluctant to change, for fear of becoming selfish. What, as you see it, is the difference between being assertive and being selfish?

On the Unity of Life

When I spoke with my friend about the unique nature of the pain that I had experienced upon my father's death, my friend said, "That is exactly the way that I felt when my father died."

On the Unity of Life

Humans everywhere are vastly similar to one another—we all use language to communicate, experience similar fears, dream dreams, procreate via sexual intercourse, display the same six basic emotions, choose official and unofficial leaders, develop rituals, celebrate holidays, encourage long-term relationships, and set aside certain individuals for the tasks of ministry and healing. Yet we continue to divide people into categories—to act as if "us" and "them" were meaningful distinctions.

We are all in this together, whether we realize it or not. At least once each day I want to be able to set aside my rampant egocentrism long enough to see and to experience our common humanity.

Those people who see theology and psychology as being contradictory do not really understand either one.

Those people who see sexuality and spirituality as being contradictory do not really understand either one, either.

Where some people tend to see barriers, divisions, or differences, I tend to see intersections, overlap, and similarities. For example, although major wars have been fought in the name of religious differences, it seems to me that most of the religions in the world have asked fundamentally the same questions—"Why are we here?" "What types of relationships are we to have with one another and with God?" "What happens to us when we die?"—and have arrived at answers that, despite the superficial differences that their proponents often stress, are in fact fundamentally the same.

One advantage of seeing similarities rather than differences is that it helps to free me from the need to reject all of those people who are "different."

Another advantage of seeing similarities is that it helps me to connect with people. As Carl Rogers pointed out, that which is most personal is most universal; at our deepest level, we all are very similar to one another. Thus, if I choose to focus on the differences between myself and someone else, I can interact with that person only on a rather superficial level, whereas if I choose to focus on the ways in which I am fundamentally similar to the other person, I can connect in a very powerful way.

Whenever I truly connect with someone, the experience heals us both.

It is so clear to me: the feeling that I get when I truly connect with someone and the feeling that I get when I experience God's presence are exactly the same feeling. To be in touch with another person's essence is to stand in the presence of God.

No matter how educated, powerful, or famous I become, at the deepest level of my being I still will be exactly the same as everyone else.

True humility does not involve putting oneself down; it is not synonymous with low self-esteem. True humility springs not from the belief that we somehow are less than everyone else, but rather from the knowledge that at the deepest level we are the same as everyone else.

I am exactly as important as every other person in the world, and I never will be all that important to the world until I understand and embrace that fact.

Although our differences may seem striking at first, in truth it is our similarities that are the most profound.

It now is easier for me to understand how God could love each of us to precisely the same degree.

Oftentimes, it is the people who appear to be the exact opposites of one another who are, in fact, the most similar.

As soon as we choose to focus on our differences rather than on our similarities, we begin to compete with each other for the honor of being best.

We cannot love someone with whom we are competing.

Questions for personal reflection

1. Think of a person who seems to be very different from you. Now try to list at least twelve ways in which the two of you are the same.

2. Which specific persons are causing you the greatest difficulty right now? If you were to remember how similar they were to you, how might that change the relationships?

3. If you were to choose always to focus on the ways in which you were similar to everyone else, what effect might that decision have on your emotional life? Your spiritual life?

On Acceptance
and Forgiveness

The moment I accept my own forgiveness,
I see how ludicrous have been all of my
attempts to judge others.

On Acceptance and Forgiveness

Accepting and forgiving ourselves

Although they use slightly different words to make the point, psychologists and Christians agree that the process of change begins the instant that we feel accepted and forgiven. Psychologists and Christians also agree that we can experience acceptance and forgiveness only if we first acknowledge our need for forgiveness. Thus, telling ourselves the truth, already mentioned as a precondition for growth, triggers the experience of acceptance and forgiveness, which in turn triggers the coming into being of our new selves.

I am seriously flawed and I want to simply acknowledge that fact, instead of rationalizing it away, so that I might come to accept myself and thereby be healed.

Change becomes possible in the instant that I acknowledge who I am; my future begins the moment I embrace the present.

People who have undergone near-death experiences often have reported that God did indeed review with them the good points and bad points of their lives on earth, prior to their going to heaven. Apparently, even after we die, the same rule still holds true—change begins only when we acknowledge that which has gone before.

Many religions seem to assume that the goal of religion is to get people to feel badly about themselves—to destroy their last shred of self-esteem. As I see it, however, while we do indeed need to acknowledge our flaws, we do so not as an end in itself, but as a means to an end; not because there is any value in endlessly beating ourselves up, but because each of us wants eventually to become a new being.

Although I ought never to belabor the fact that I am sinful and imperfect, I ought never to forget it, either.

Before I can forgive myself or experience God's forgiveness of me, I first must acknowledge that I am in need of forgiveness. Trying to rationalize away my behavior never works, because I never can forgive myself for a crime that I am pretending not to have committed.

I ought never to engage in an excess of self-condemnation, either, for that blocks God's ability to communicate with me. As I see it, God's message to us generally is two-fold: God forgives us for our past mistakes and challenges us to do better in the future. When I wallow in self-blame, I cannot hear the first half of the message and I am unable to respond to the second.

Before I can see myself as I am, I must be willing to look rather carefully at my life.

Self-examination is not a group process. Thus, if I am to look closely at myself, I need to spend some time alone.

If I have the TV or stereo cranked up, it does not qualify as alone time.

To many people, the prospect of spending time alone in order to see oneself more clearly is frightening because they are afraid that when they see themselves clearly they will not like the person they see.

Luckily, this fear is unfounded.

All the people I know who have made a point of spending some time with themselves have come away from that experience with new appreciation for their own inner beauty. This makes a lot of sense to me. After all, God resides at the core of each of us. Thus, the more carefully we look at ourselves, the more clearly we will see the beautiful child of God that resides within each of us.

Questions for personal reflection

1. What are some of the flaws that you have had difficulty acknowledging?

2. How has this lack of acknowledgment affected your life? How has it affected the lives of the people around you?

3. Acknowledging your flaws out loud, in the presence of at least one other human being, can be tremendously healing. With whom might you feel safe doing this?

4. When you look back on your life, whose forgiveness would you most like to receive? Is it possible to tell the person(s) involved how you feel?

5. Spend some time alone asking yourself who you really are and what it is that you want to do with your life. What sorts of answers begin to occur to you?

On Acceptance and Forgiveness

Accepting and forgiving others

While we are called to examine carefully our own lives, it definitely is not our job to be anyone else's judge, a point the scriptures (Matthew 7:5, Luke 6:37, Romans 14:10, and James 4:12) and the AA injunctions against "taking someone else's inventory" make very clear. Judging others simply does not work; we cannot change people by condemning them. In fact, our judgments are likely to solidify their defensive posture, to the point that change becomes impossible.

If we truly want to help people, if we want to become for them an instrument of change, then we must accept them as they are. It is our love and acceptance, not our acts of condemnation, that will create for them the possibility of healing.

My judgments of others, my desires to punish or to seek revenge, and my manipulative attempts to force people to change all serve no useful purpose. I want to let go of all of these and to instead offer to people exactly what I would wish to receive from them— gentleness, understanding, and the kind of forgiving love that heals all of my wounds.

To accept others does not require any special effort. Rather, it requires a certain lack of effort.

If we wish to accept others, we need only to refrain from expending all of the energy that usually goes into judging people and all of the effort that usually goes into rationalizing those judgements.

To love and to accept others is our natural state; it is all else that is unnatural.

Every minute that I have spent judging someone else is a minute of my life that I have totally wasted.

The less I judge others, the less I worry about their judgments of me.

When I judge others, I distance myself not only from that other person but also from God, who is a God of forgiveness.

Judging creates distance. Perhaps this is why those people who are uncomfortable with emotional closeness tend to be so critical of others.

The opposite of intimacy is judgment.

I should indeed strive to love my enemies, not because it necessarily will make any difference to them, but because it will free me.

Whenever I forgive someone, the one who invariably gets healed is me.

Whenever I refuse to forgive someone, the one who invariably pays the price for that refusal is me.

My desire to hurt someone always hurts me the most of all.

Questions for personal reflection

1. Who are the people in your life who are particularly difficult for you to forgive? What effect has this lack of forgiveness had upon your life?

2. At those times when you notice that you are not truly accepting or forgiving someone, what are you usually doing instead? What would it take for you to quit doing that?

3. If after trying to implement your ideas from #2, you still have trouble forgiving someone, consider the following four questions:

   a. "Am I acting as if I never could have done such a thing?" If so, you may wish to remind yourself that the other person probably is a lot like you.

b. "Am I having trouble forgiving myself for similar offenses that I have committed or been tempted to commit in the past?" If so, you may wish to begin working harder on self-acceptance—on accepting yourself, flaws and all.

c. "Am I blocking my ability to forgive by continually reminding myself of the person's past offenses?" If so, you may want to strive to leave yourself more open to the present, which is always new.

d. "Is there an intense emotion, such as anger, that I have suppressed and from which I therefore have never recovered?" If so, you may want to acknowledge and express that emotion, in safe ways and places, so that it gradually loses its power over you and quits blocking your ability to move on.

On Being Vulnerable

We men spend a lot of our time protecting ourselves. The question is, protecting ourselves against what?

On Being Vulnerable

Our fear of self-revelation

To be intimate (by which I do not mean merely being sexual) with another person is to be able to say to that person, through our actions and our words, "This is who I am." Thus, an intimate relationship requires that we make our true selves known; it requires meaningful self-revelation. If we are to be intimate with another human being, it is not enough for us to talk with that person only about trivia or about such safe topics as the weather, our favorite football team, the children, or the perceived inadequacies of a co-worker. We must be willing to talk about ourselves—we must be willing to let that other person see inside of us.

Of course, this is risky, because when we let other people know and care about us, it creates the possibility of being hurt. However, it also creates the possibility of being loved for who we really are, an experience that has the power to transform our lives. So, the choice is simple: either we can continue to protect ourselves, with the full knowledge that we are thereby condemning ourselves to a life devoid of any real meaning, or we can take a chance in the hopes of obtaining life's greatest prize.

I know that there can be no real intimacy in my relationships as long as I continue to hide behind my "I've got it all together" mask. I want to let people see the real me—the person who has strong feelings, who messes up some times, who dreams crazy dreams, and who cares deeply about others.

The strong silent type is not really strong at all. Gutless, yes; strong, no.

The most selfish act in the world is to care deeply about someone without ever letting that person know.

To rationalize my fear of self-revelation is to miss this fundamental point: there is more to life than simply protecting myself against pain.

Way down inside of me, protected by my many defenses, is the part of me that I now call the vulnerable one. Although the vulnerable one is very afraid of being known, I gradually am finding that much of that fear is unfounded; I am finding that the protector, the one who guards my hurting self, simply is not as important as he had led me to believe.

When I talk with other men about my vulnerable one, I almost always find that they too have such a one deep inside of them. We may call it by different names and may protect it in slightly different ways, but everything else is the same; we all feel a deep sense of sadness or hurt that we never have expressed, we all feel quite vulnerable in the face of that sadness, we all work far too hard to protect that vulnerable part of ourselves, and we all long for a time when things could be different.

In my counseling practice I occasionally encounter a truly stereotypic male. Whenever I do, I never know whether to laugh or to cry. On the one hand, his attempts to defend himself against the possibility of an intimate relationship (for example, his surface toughness, his monosyllabic responses to my questions, and his tendency to fix things rather than to listen) are so obvious that I almost have to laugh, despite my frustration. On the other hand, however, the consequences of his protective habits (for example, his suffocating isolation, his painful lack of spontaneity, and his apparent inability to truly enjoy life) are equally obvious and often move me to tears, despite his awkward attempts to prevent me from caring for him.

The problem with the stereotypical male, then, is precisely this: the things that he most desperately needs to receive are also the things against which he is the most heavily defended.

I am far from being a stereotypical male, yet I too defend myself unnecessarily against precisely that which I most need to experience.

The clumsy ways in which we protect ourselves would be laughable if the results were not so painful.

We need each other desperately, whether we wish to acknowledge that fact or not.

My fear of intimacy is not about giving, it is about receiving.

To be a receiver is to not be in control.

Thus, if I am to get better at intimacy, I must also get better at relinquishing my perceived need for control.

Some men use sex as a way to avoid intimacy, rather than as a way to enhance intimacy. They engage in casual sexual encounters so that they can satisfy their aching need to be in a relationship without having to engage in the scary business of meaningful self-revelation. Unfortunately for them, they all eventually discover that their experiences have served only to reinforce the sense of isolation and alienation that motivated their behavior in the first place.

Using another human in this way never works, because it reduces the other person to an object, and objects never can satisfy our need for intimacy.

People can save us. Objects cannot.

Questions for personal reflection

1. What is it that you are most in need of receiving from other people? What has prevented you from receiving this in the past?

2. People need to be intelligently vulnerable. While we should indeed be more revealing of ourselves, we also need to be a bit careful about that—we need to pick our spots. If you wanted to begin to share more of yourself, when and with whom might you start? (Note—Try to start with the easiest person rather than with the hardest or the most important. Start small and work your way up.)

On Being Vulnerable

Our fear of sadness

Time and time again, in my own life and in my work with my clients, I have found that sadness seems to be our most deeply buried emotion. When people have undergone some sort of traumatic childhood experience, for example, they first are likely to deny that the experience occurred. Oftentimes, it is only years later, after they have acknowledged the reality of what occurred, that they can allow themselves to feel angry about it. And only after that, sometimes long after that, do the tears come. I have noticed that we tend to deal with death in the same way: we begin with denial, then we progress to being angry at God, and only later do we eventually allow ourselves to feel the deep grief and sadness that precede acceptance.

I am not entirely sure why it is that sadness comes last, but I suspect that it is at least partly because sadness is the emotion that leaves us feeling the most vulnerable. It does not energize us the way happiness can, nor does it create the feeling of power that our self-righteous anger can generate. Instead, it leaves us feeling small and unprotected—alone in a world that can be harsh and frightening.

I am sure that I am sad about some things that I do not even know that I am sad about. I want to be able to acknowledge and to experience that sadness, so that I might finally be healed.

Many of us men have difficulty expressing various emotions, but I do not think that any of our emotions are as difficult for us to express as are our feelings of hurt/loss/sadness.

A famous therapist once commented that he never had met a man who did not carry around with him some profound, unresolved feelings of grief. That comment itself caused me to experience a great deal of grief.

How do we get over sadness? By letting ourselves feel sad.

When I quit fighting against feeling sad, I eventually quit feeling so sad.

Happiness never lasts because we do not fight it. The same is true of our sadness, once we quit fighting that.

Even if I do not know why exactly it is that I am feeling so sad, I still can accept the feeling, allow myself to experience it, and then move on.

Questions for personal reflection

1. What are your deepest hurts? What techniques do you use to guard against feeling and expressing these hurts?

2. What do you fear will happen if you do experience and exhibit these feelings?

3. What will happen if you do not?

On Relationships

It is not my task in life to make sure that everyone likes me. My task, rather, is to find those people that I like and to spend as much time with them as I can. Life is a treasure hunt, not a popularity contest.

On Relationships

Our relationships with our partners and friends

It seems to me that men tend to make three basic mistakes when it comes to relationships. The first mistake is to assume that our need to develop an intimate relationship with our partners ends once we "have" them. The second mistake is to assume that our partners can and should fulfill all of our needs for intimacy. The third mistake is to confuse intimacy with sexuality, to the point that our partners become reluctant to express any feelings of closeness, for fear that we will mistakenly interpret that as a sign that they want to have intercourse.

*I want to make my relationship with my wife,
Gwen, an ongoing priority, I want to seek out
intimate relationships with other men and women
as well, and I want always to remember that there
are many, many ways to express affection.*

To know love is to want to share it; to have it is to want to give it away.

Gwen's love for me has helped me to learn how to love my friends.

The more that I get in touch with my love for all people, the less that I need any one individual. I find this fact to be both liberating and frightening.

I never had any women who were truly my friends until I quit worrying about categories and about "where this is going."

In my relationships with men, I do not ask, "Where is this going." I just ask myself, "How is this going, so far?" and then act accordingly. Now, in my relationships with women, I also just ask myself, "How is this going, so far?" and then act accordingly.

A relationship is a relationship is a relationship.

Hugh Prather pointed out in his book *Notes to Myself* (Real People Press, 1970) that when we distance ourselves from someone it is because we see something in that person which we dislike in ourselves. I agree, and I think that it also is true that when we are attracted to someone it is because we see something in the person that we would like to see in ourselves. I was attracted to Gwen, in part, because she was in many ways the kind of person that I always had wanted to be; she had made actual much of what still was only potential in me.

The ways in which our partners are different from us can enrich the relationship, as long as we are willing to respect and admire those differences.

It is not our job to force our partners to become more like us. Our job, rather, is to admire our partners and seek to become more like them.

Couples generally do not split up because the bad times are so bad. Rather, they split up because the good times just are not that good.

Luckily, most of the good things that happen in a relationship (going on dates, exchanging little gifts, being silly, spending quiet time together, making love, listening carefully to each other, sharing each other's joys and sorrows, vacationing together) are within our power to control.

An on-again, off-again relationship suggests a conflict between fantasy and reality.

It seems to me that extramarital affairs are primarily about interpersonal distance; they are an attempt either to overcome it or to create it.

Although people often equate sex with love, in truth it is only in the very best of relationships that the two overlap.

We men tend to move too quickly in relationships, which hinders our ability to experience this overlap.

There should be some sort of test that you have to pass before you can call it making love.

All too often, the people who desperately need a chance to experience love without sex end up settling for sex without love.

Questions for personal reflection

1. How much of your time do you spend with people whose company you truly enjoy? How might you increase this amount?

2. If you knew yourself to be capable of loving and being loved by all people, how might that affect your current relationship(s)?

3. Who among your friends and acquaintances has the potential to become a more intimate friend? How might you begin that process?

4. Think of a person to whom you are attracted. What quality or qualities does the person exhibit that you also would like to exhibit? How might that person be of help to you in this regard?

On Relationships

Our relationships with our children

Our relationships with our children are different from our other relationships in at least two fundamental ways. First, in any parent-child relationship there exists a tremendous power differential. This inequality of power means that we must be careful never to treat our young children as our friends or confidants, that we must be very careful as to how we express our anger, and that it is unrealistic to expect the child to be the one who initiates a change in the relationship.

The second unique characteristic of a parent-child relationship is the ultimate goal of the relationship—to enable our children to leave us. Given that this is our goal, it is important that we neither pamper our children nor force them always to do things our way, for both of these interfere with the process of their becoming responsible adults.

I want to give to my child all of the things that I would give to an intimate friend of mine, while always remembering that my child is not my friend.

The parent-child relationship contains within it an irony that few of us parents ever want to acknowledge. When we do a poor job of raising our children, they hang around forever, hoping against hope that they finally will gain our approval. Conversely, if we do a good job of raising our children, then as soon as they are grown they go off to start a new life of their own.

To fail is to be constantly reminded of one's failure, and to succeed is to lose one's little child forever.

The problem with living one's life totally for others is that it makes it very difficult to let people go.

The empty nest syndrome is our problem, not theirs.

As a parent, it is indeed my job to look after my child, but it is not her job to look after me.

Parenting is not a two-way street; unlike a relationship between equals, it is almost totally about giving, and only very secondarily about receiving.

It seems to me that most young parents have children for the wrong reason—not because they want to give something, but because they want to get something.

If you feel that your children never talk to you, ask yourself this: do you ever talk to them?

It is not enough to say, "I am always ready to listen." We have to talk honestly about ourselves first, and *then* be ready to listen.

Although it is easy to make a child the scapegoat, our children never can be solely to blame for what is wrong with the family, because they do not have the power in the family—we do.

Questions for personal reflection

1. To what extent did your parents allow you to be a child?

2. To what extent do you allow your children to be children? Do you see the need for any changes here?

3. We have difficulty letting go of our children, in part, because we are afraid of what might happen if we do. What are you afraid might happen if you were to allow your children to make more of their own decisions? How does this fear affect your relationship with your children?

On Perfectionism
and Workaholism

*Despite my best efforts to prove otherwise,
the fact remains that life just is not that
serious a business.*

On Perfectionism and Workaholism

We perfectionists and workaholics tend to be people who feel that we are not good enough and who strive to overcome that internal feeling through the piling up of impressive external accomplishments. Of course, this never works—the feeling always persists. This leads us to conclude that we apparently need to work even harder or to do it even better if we are ever to feel that we are good enough. And so is born the exhausting treadmill to nowhere, a treadmill that ends only when we realize that no external achievement exists that is capable of filling a hole in our soul.

I want always to remember that I am more than what I do and that not everything in life that is worth doing is worth doing well.

One problem with my perfectionism is that it so radically limits the new activities that I can try.

Perfectionism originates not in the desire to gain approval but rather in the desire to avoid criticism.

When people are deathly afraid of criticism, they begin to define successful interactions not in terms of what happens but in terms of what does not; the best that can be hoped for is the absence of any negative feedback. This is why perfectionists are not happy people.

This also is why perfectionists tend to stifle all meaningful conversation.

We all say things like "nobody is perfect," and then we turn around and pretend to be the only exception.

The only thing harder than playing God is acknowledging the fact that I am not God.

Pretending to be a perfect human is just as dangerous as pretending to be God.

Successful people are not people who never fail. Rather, they are people who, when they do fail, openly acknowledge their failure and then begin their search for a new way.

The problem with workaholics is that they never work on the truly important tasks.

Whenever I get too caught up in my work or in thinking that I have to complete a certain project, my little girl walks into the room, smiles at me, and wordlessly reminds me of the things that truly are important.

I do want to do something that matters; the question is, matters to whom?

It is unfortunate that we in our culture tend to put so much emphasis on finishing things, since so few things ever are really finished.

If I were less compulsive about completion, I probably would be more aware of life's beauty.

If I want to better understand my life, I need to be willing to step out of it from time to time.

My periods of activity are most productive when they are interspersed with periods of inactivity. I get the most done when I have just gotten done doing nothing.

It is precisely at those times when I least can afford to take a vacation that I most desperately need to do so.

I am not saying that we ought never to work hard. I am, after all, a person who works very hard at what he does. What I am saying is that my life has real meaning only when it has balance and that workaholics, by definition, lack balance.

The importance of balance is evidenced by the pain and unhappiness that I feel as soon as my life gets out of balance.

Questions for personal reflection

1. In what way(s) and in what area(s) do you pretend to be perfect? What price do you pay for these pretenses?

2. What are you afraid will happen when you fail? What actually did happen the last time that you failed?

3. If you suddenly felt that you had permission to fail, what new activities might you try?

4. What are the activities that you could start doing or go back to doing that would help to add balance to your life?

On Personal
and Spiritual Growth

*I learn the most at those times when no
one is talking.*

On Personal and Spiritual Growth

Getting started

Growth starts with a decision: the decision to look honestly at one's life, to acknowledge what we see, and to begin changing the parts that we do not like. Thus, although the growth process tends to be a gradual one, the process can be *started* in an instant; I can decide right now that I want to begin making some important changes in my life.

When I first begin to implement some of these changes, I often will feel a bit awkward. This is perfectly natural; whether I am learning how to play basketball, drive a car, knit a sweater, or communicate more effectively with my partner, I always will feel a bit awkward at the beginning. So, I need to remember that this awkwardness is normal—that it is not a sign that I am "doing it wrong."

I want to have the courage to acknowledge those things that I know are in need of change and I want to persevere until the changes have become a natural part of my new self.

It seems to me that the cruelest people in the world are those who are too frightened to change.

Often, when one person in a family starts getting healthy, the others respond by getting angry.

Sometimes, when I point out to my clients the fact that they will need to start making certain changes in their lives, they respond by saying something like "Oh, that will be so hard." Now, whenever I hear that, I ask, "Has the easy way made you happy?"

Life often presents me with a choice between the easy way and the right way.

The problem with the easy way out is that it never really is.

To consistently choose the easy way is to eventually be stuck with a very small life.

Sometimes people say to me, "I can't change; this is just my personality." It seems to me, though, that a personality is simply an established pattern of decisions or a consistent way of making decisions and that we always can choose to start making different decisions.

One reason why it is difficult for us humans to choose to grow is that our maladaptive responses often are quite effective, at least in the short run.

As an adolescent, I always was uncomfortable with closeness. I therefore became quite sarcastic. In the short run, this maladaptive response worked quite well; it kept people at a distance and thus helped me to reduce my level of discomfort. Of course, my sarcasm did nothing to alleviate the long-term problem. In fact, it probably served to increase its severity: the better I became at keeping people at a distance, the more uncomfortable I felt on those occasions when I did have to hold up my end of a meaningful conversation.

Ironically, we often are unable to grow unless we are willing to give up the one response we have that works.

I cannot learn how to walk in a whole new way unless I am willing to stumble for a while first.

There are two very different ways of getting into a swimming pool, and both are perfectly acceptable.

I, like many Americans, tend to think in terms of the quick fix. Once I have a goal clearly in mind, I want to achieve it immediately. This generally leads to much unhappiness and dissatisfaction, since real change often is gradual.

Achieving my goal is nowhere near as important as getting started; it is the *direction* of my journey that is most important.

To grow older is to be faced with one of life's most fundamental questions: Am I going to clutch tightly onto what I already know, do, and believe, or am I going to leave myself open to new possibilities?

Questions for personal reflection

1. In what area(s) would you most like to grow?

2. What (relatively effective) response(s) might you have to give up in order to achieve this?

3. What will you gain when you do?

4. What will you lose if you do not?

On Personal and Spiritual Growth

The process of growth

Growth is a slow, life-long process. Thus, if I am to be committed to personal and spiritual growth, I must be willing to be patient, I must continually replace my previously accomplished goals with ever-higher ones, and I must always remember that growth is a way of life, not a task that we get to finish.

I want to strive to drop my need for instant gratification and to commit myself instead to a life-style based on becoming.

Personal growth is a subtractive process, not an additive one. It does not require the development of a new or different personality. Rather, it requires only that we be willing to whittle away all those parts of our personality that never were ours to begin with.

People in the process of growing are not like painters applying fresh paint to a previously blank canvas. They are, rather, like sculptors who slowly chip away all of the unnecessary stone in order to reveal the beautiful person who had been in there all along.

To grow is to gradually drop all of our pretenses.

We do not grow into somebody else. Rather, we grow into ourselves.

If I am to be actively engaged in the process of growth, I must be willing to jettison other people's preconceived notions of who I am so that I might gradually discover who I really am.

For me, to be moving toward wholeness is to be moving beyond the limits and definitions that have been imposed upon me by others.

When I believe that I am only what other people think that I am or when I try always to be the person that I believe other people want me to be, I lose the chance to become myself.

Every once in a while, I get a blinding insight into my own life. I suddenly understand, with perfect clarity, why I act or feel the way that I do. This vivid glimpse of the real me always excites me, but it always startles me, too.

To be face-to-face with my real self is both exhilarating and frightening.

Questions for personal reflection

1. Which parts of your current self would you like to whittle away?

2. Who do other people think that you are? Who would you like to be, instead?

3. When you suddenly come face-to-face with yourself, what do you see? What parts do you like? What parts do you dislike?

On Personal and Spiritual Growth

The outcomes of growth

As I grow, I tend to become more true to my real self, less concerned with what others think, more at peace with myself, and less concerned about the rules. Thus, I become not more conventional but more unconventional, not more of a conformist but more of a nonconformist. This is why the people in history who have functioned at the highest possible level always have been viewed by others as being rather dangerous.

To be a human is to be in the midst of change. I want to embrace the changes that occur in my life and to be of help to others who find themselves increasingly at odds with convention.

The maturing process can be a funny thing—often, by the time that I finally can have the possession, job, or opportunity that I always wanted, I no longer want it.

In the past, I almost always have judged my actions by their consequences. The more that I grow, however, the more able I am to judge my actions without reference to these external (and highly unreliable) signs of success or failure.

The more I grow, the more able I am to evaluate myself according to the process, rather than the outcome.

My primary reasons for doing things are changing. At one time in my life, I taught, wrote, and counseled primarily for external reasons—because of the positive ways in which other people treated me when I performed those tasks. I still teach, write, and do counseling. Now, however, I engage in these tasks primarily for internal reasons—because they are among the activities that best express (and thus bring me closest to) my essence. Now I do them because when I do, God and I are one.

Personal growth is mostly about why, rather than what.

The people who are at the highest level of human development are not those who have separated themselves from their "lower" functions, nor are they the people who act as if they are slaves to those functions. Rather, they are the people who consistently can integrate those lower functions with their "higher" selves.

When we make love with our partner in a way that expresses both the intensity of our desire and the depth of our love, we can catch a glimpse of what that highest level of human development must be like.

When I feel as comfortable with my "baser" drives as I do with my "purer" ones, I will know that I have arrived.

The more that I grow, the more willing that I am to break the rules. Perhaps this is why those Christians who have a strong need to enforce the rules (that is, to impose their set of rules upon all others) always have been so irritating to me—they are trying to convert other people to Christianity, while they themselves are deathly afraid of its true consequences.

Jesus ate with tax collectors, talked intimately with ostracized women, and healed people on the Sabbath. Obviously, he was incorrigible.

Other people can provide me with opinions, insights, and facts, but only I can decide what is right for me. No matter how tempting it is to give away my power or to live by someone else's rules, the fact remains: no one else can be my judge.

Of course, this means that I cannot be anyone else's judge, either.

When people get healthier they quit blaming and they start helping.

I will have achieved true beauty when my presence helps to bring out the beauty in everyone around me.

The past is both immediately over and forever with us. No one who knew me as the clumsy, nonverbal, virtually invisible child that I once was would believe how relaxed and comfortable I now am with myself and with other people. Yet even now I squirm in my chair when people pay too much attention to me.

Questions for personal reflection

1. What are some of the possessions, jobs, or opportunities that you once wanted that you no longer want?

2. What are some of the *whys* that have changed for you as you have grown?

3. What are some of the rules that you will have to be willing to break if you are to continue growing?

4. What aspects of your past self have you left behind? What parts still are with you?

On Religion

*Religion is a tricky thing; I know lots of
people who are very serious about their
faith and who still manage, somehow, to
miss the whole point.*

On Religion

Our religion is not supposed to be based on our insecurities. Thus, I have no patience with those who pander to other people's fears or with those whose own insecurities lead them to want everybody else to agree with them. Our faith, whether we are Christian, Muslim, Jew, Taoist, or whatever, is to be built upon a rock—the sure knowledge of God—not upon our fears, doubts, and insecurities. Anything less than that is a sham and does a disservice to ourselves, to others, and to God.

I want never to settle for a prepackaged faith distributed by people who are unsure of their own relationship with God, and I want always to be true to the God who is revealed to me every time that I pray.

There are all too many religions whose proponents would lead us to believe that God will love us only if we follow all of the rules laid down by that particular religious sect.

God did not start to love me when I became a Christian; rather, I became a Christian only when I realized that God loved me.

It was only when I stopped trying to earn God's love that I was able to accept the fact that God had loved me all along.

God does not love us because. God just loves us.

If sinlessness were the price of God's love, none of us could afford to buy it.

God's love is not something that we can win. Luckily, it is not something that we can lose, either.

We humans so often get things backwards—we think that God will love us only if we do all of the *right things,* whereas in truth it is only when we realize that God loves us that we are enabled to do all of the right things.

Loving behavior is a heartfelt response, not an opening gambit.

The world probably would be a better place if we all quit trying to earn God's love and if we tried instead simply to cherish the gift.

For me, the state of being closely connected to God has at least one thing in common with my intimate relationship with my wife—as soon as I quit working on it, I lose it.

God's love is indeed a free gift, but staying in touch with that gift requires a consistent effort on my part.

What determines the rightness or wrongness of a particular act is not so much the act itself but the reason for that act.

It seems to me that many people's moral codes are too simplistic, in that they consist of a list of *dos* and *don'ts,* rather than a list of *whys* and *why nots.*

All too often, I hear people (especially young people) define the success of their outreach efforts in terms of the number of converts that they have acquired. It seems to me, though, that a Christian's job (a job that has not changed since Jesus first held the position) is not to convert people but to preach and live the Good News. We are to be judged by the process, not by the results.

Our task is not to force people to respond but rather to provide them with the opportunity to respond. As Jesus said, "He who has ears, let him hear." (Mark 4:9)

Everywhere we look, we find proof of God's preference for diversity. For example, there are many different life forms (animals, for example), many different varieties of each particular life form (dogs, for example), many different species within each variety (collies, for example), and many individual variations between members of a particular species. All of this adds up to a world filled with countless billions of unique expressions of life.

Given God's obvious preference for diversity, our search for the one true religion seems silly at best, and contrary to God's will at worst.

God loves diversity. It is only we humans who yearn for uniformity—witness the difference between a planted field and a natural woodland.

My faith literally heals me, because to believe in new possibilities is to begin to make actual those possibilities.

My life is limited only by my unbelief.

One of the hardest things in life to accept is the fact that sometimes there is no reason. As the writer of Ecclesiastes said, "I saw that under the sun the race is not to the swift, . . . But time and chance happen to them all." (Ecclesiastes 9:11)

Acceptance is not a passive act, nor a simple one.

Questions for personal reflection

1. In what ways do you try to earn the love of God and of others? If God were to appear to you and to tell you how unnecessary this was, how would you feel?

2. When you get to the point in your life where you truly know, at the core of your being, that God loves you, how will that change the way in which you treat others? How might you begin to implement at least some of those changes right now?

3. What would be your *whys* and *why nots* if you were to draw up your own personal code of morality?

4. What have been the hardest things in life for you to accept? Are there any ways in which God and/or the other people in your life could help you with these?

On God

God is both powerful and peaceful, which sounds like a contradiction, but is not.

On God

Every one of God's messengers, from Lao Tsu to the Jewish prophets to Jesus to Mohammed, has been frustrated by the human tendency to see God as someone who lives, acts, thinks, and evaluates in the same ways that we do. All of these messengers, in their own ways, tried to tell us (some would say, warn us) just how wrong we were. All of them tried to shock us into understanding that God's rules and our rules are not the same and that anyone who is a slave to the human rules eventually will find himself or herself in opposition to God's will.

I am not sure that we understand the message any better today than did the people who so frustrated God's earlier messengers. All of our major religions were founded by people who understood the importance of breaking society's rules, and yet everywhere I go I encounter people who seem to believe that it is their job to enforce society's rules on others, all in the name of their religion.

If Jesus were to return to the earth today, he undoubtedly would be crucified all over again. And the mob once again would be led by those religious people pompous and self-righteous enough to assume that God's rules were the same as theirs.

God, I know that although you love me, you are not like me; I know that your ways are not my ways. I want always to remember that your thoughts, your way of perceiving people, and the timetable on which you operate all are qualitatively different from mine.

It seems to me that most of our misguided views of God are misguided precisely because they are based on the assumption that God is nothing more than a larger version of ourselves.

God is both contained within me and yet totally other— hence the inadequacy of any theology that assumes that God is merely a very large human.

The fact that I can have a personal relationship with God does not imply that God is a person.

The love of God is a lot stronger than our petty human rules of conduct.

People tend to spend a lot of time feeling guilty about things that God could not care less about.

The fact that nature does operate in certain organized, lawful ways has led some people to write lengthy tomes that purport to systematically describe all of the dimensions of life. It seems to me, though, that there is an essential mystery to life that threads its way through all of our experiences and that we cannot systematically explain or adequately describe.

While I can rationally explain the healing effects of love, I cannot explain love.

"As you do not know how the spirit comes to the bones in the womb of a woman with child, so you do not know the work of God." (Ecclesiastes 11:5)

The more highly developed my view of God becomes, the less I can (or want to) explain everything and the fewer absolute statements I can make.

The better I understand who I am, who God is, and who we are together, the less I feel the need to convince everyone that I am right (and the more convincing I become).

God is like a rippling lake—a lot of motion on the surface and a great calmness underneath.

At those times when I am most closely connected to God, my actions, too, are rooted in a fundamental calmness.

I once saw a poster that advised people to act like ducks— to remain calm on the surface and to paddle like heck underneath. It seems to me, though, that God calls us to do exactly the opposite—to be outwardly active, while remaining inwardly calm.

People often say things like "When I was ready, God created such and such an opportunity for me." It seems to me, though, that it would be more accurate to say, "God repeatedly has made such and such an opportunity available to me, and when I was ready I finally chose to avail myself of that opportunity."

Always the light is with us.

The presence of clouds, fog, unhappiness, or other temporary conditions ought never to be confused with the absence of light.

I cannot see the light unless my eyes are open.

Questions for personal reflection

1. What are the times, places, or activities that help you to become more aware of God's presence in your life? What might you do to increase the frequency of those experiences?

2. If you took seriously God's otherness and lack of regard for our petty human rules, how might that change your concept of God? How might it change your behavior?

3. What are some of the ways in which God has been active in your life?

4. What have these encounters taught you about the nature of God?

An Invitation

My work as a counselor and spiritual director has helped to convince me that my role in life has to do not with endings but with beginnings—with helping people to begin the process of learning, loving, healing, and reconciliation.

This book, then, is intended to serve not as an ending but as a beginning; not as a conclusion but as an invitation. My prayer for you is that you will consciously choose this day to start the life-long process of growing into your own gentle self— a self whose honesty, wisdom, and capacity for intimacy will serve to inspire and to heal all of those whose lives you touch.

May you never stop becoming.

—Glenn

Whole Person Associates

Whole Person Associates publishes materials focused on stress management, wellness promotion, and personal growth. Our structured exercises for workshops and groups, relaxation audiotapes, workshops-in-a-book, and interactive video programs are designed for personal and professional use. Trainers, consultants, educators, therapists, psychologists, and wellness coordinators use our products in hospitals, corporate wellness programs, health care facilities, EAPs, colleges, drug and alcohol abuse programs, and in private practice. Call or write for our free catalog.

Whole Person Associates Inc
210 West Michigan
Duluth, MN 55802-1908
(218) 727-0500